COOPERATION

by Janet Riehecky
illustrated by Kathryn Hutton

THE CHILD'S WORLD

Mankato, MN 56001

Jack Sprat could eat no fat.
His wife could eat no lean;
And so betwixt the two of them,
They licked the platter clean.

—Mother Goose

Library of Congress Cataloging in Publication Data

Riehecky, Janet, 1953-
  Cooperation / by Janet Riehecky ; illustrated by Kathryn Hutton.
      p. cm.
  Summary: Portrays situations illustrating the importance of
cooperation.
  ISBN 0-89565-565-9
  1. Cooperation (Ethics)—Juvenile literature.
[1. Cooperativeness.]   I. Hutton, Kathryn, ill.   II. Title.
BJ1474.R54   1990
179'.9—dc20
                                                  89-48284
                                                    CIP
                                                    AC

What is cooperation? Cooperation is
working together to get something
done.

It's holding the boards for your new playhouse while your dad hammers them together . . .

and working together with your
friends to finish it up.

Cooperation is pushing the back of the wagon while your brother pulls the front . . .

and pushing up on the seesaw so your
brother can go down.

Working together to build the biggest
tower in the world is cooperation.

And so is cleaning up together after
you knock the tower down.

When you pitch and your brother
catches, that's cooperation.

Cooperation makes it easier to catch a frog . . .

paddle a canoe . . .

or make music together.

When your brother washes, your sister
dries, and you put the dishes away,
that's cooperation.

And cooperation is taking turns choosing
from the TV programs you're allowed
to watch.

When you do your best so the team
can win, that's cooperation.

And when you share your paints so everyone can make a beautiful picture, that's cooperation too.

Cooperation is building a set . . .

making costumes . . .

and learning lines—

to put on a special play.

When you and your brother decide together how your sand castle should look, that's cooperation.

Cooperation is you do one part, and
I'll do another.

It's getting the job done together.

Cooperation can make things happen!